DAVID LONGSHAW

A fashionable

children's tale for

grown-ups

FOR MAUDE

DAVID LONGSHAW
PRESENTS TO YOU,
ELEANOR AND THE SQUIRREL
(A fashionable children's tale for grown-ups.)
Written and illustrated by David Longshaw.

First   published in 2014
Text and illustrations copyright David Longshaw 2014
David Longshaw Ltd

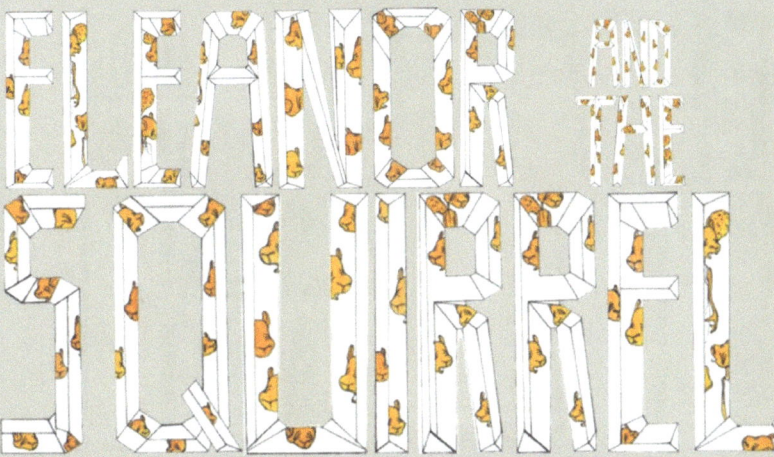

To see more of David's work – including fashion design, illustration and animation – go to:

www.davidlongshaw.co.uk

ELEANOR AND THE SQUIRREL

It was a peculiar looking thing that's for sure; I mean who dresses a squirrel in a gingham dress.

You'll have to excuse me, if I'm not quite myself, but I wanted to tell you my tale whilst the events are still fresh in my mind, before they become shrouded in myth and legend, as these things do when looking back at some of the greatest achievements.

To be honest I'm a bit hazy about the exact chain of events and some of the finer details of how everything played out in the end, I'm sure they'll come back to me over the next few days and months; but the important thing is that I am now the proud owner of this wonder of taxidermied frocked-up amazement, (to be honest I'm not even sure if it is taxidermy— it doesn't even look that much like a squirrel — it's got stitches instead of glass eyes and the fur looks more like cashmere). I'd wanted that squirrel for so long that when my grandfather finally 'gave it' to me I couldn't really remember why I had lusted after it in the first place. All I could remember is that from the very first time I saw that strange squirrel I wanted it to be mine.

I'd never really had a connection with a teddy or toy unlike Peter (my brother). He was inseparable from that funny little blue soft toy with its disproportionately large head he called Harold, I'm not even sure at the start if he was even that bothered about Harold or if it was just to keep our parents placated, they seemed to like it when he was playing with Harold. Peter usually tried to keeping them sweet so he could have time to go off on adventures in his mind.

But for me it was always about the seemingly unattainable and this time that meant the strange gingham clad squirrel.

As a child I dreamt of growing-up and one day being able to sail off with the squirrel to wondrous places. I never gave her a name, there was something more pleasing about seeing her as beyond names, to me she was more than a name, she was

The squirrel. I would often have a funny looking little bird on my head during these flights of fancy, it was terribly good at navigating and was a fount of thoughtful advice.

During my ballerina phase I imagined the squirrel and I performing in stupendous costumes on the world's greatest stages.

I would imagine myself and the squirrel as glamorous detectives solving crimes—

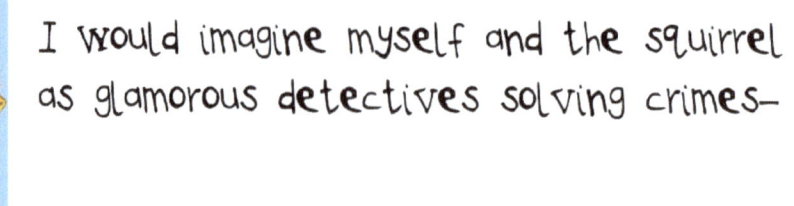

Or as spies serving queen and country

One of my favourite dreams was of
us visiting lands where
dinosaurs roamed.

I even got my mum to make me gingham dinosaur toys (as you may gather I had a thing for gingham) so I could pretend I was really there. But it was never the same, the main component was always missing.

How could I enjoy playing with the dinosaurs when I couldn't play with the squirrel?

My brother Peter had never been overly fussed about the squirrel. We were told as children that it wasn't a toy to be played with by our rather dapper grandad and Peter being Peter had heeded the warning.

That was Peter all over; other than the fact I have vague memories of visiting him in the hospital when he was born and the photographic evidence of us growing up together, I could swear that he was adopted, he didn't even look like the rest of the family.

Peter had always had a very different outlook on life. As far as Peter was concerned he was just another typical middle class boy from a middle class home. He had two loving parents and a sister (me). He lived in a nice area, in the suburbs; everything about his life was NICE. There were some ups and downs as with every family but generally life was good. And this is precisely why he knew even from a young age that no one ever writes about children like Peter, because they are boring. Their mundane lives hold no interest. They are not so incredibly poor that they have to eat their own faeces and suddenly one day something magical happens etc. etc... On the flip side, middle class boys like Peter do not live in grand palaces; they do not have wild adventures when visited by princes from afar. They live in detached/ semi-detached houses with no discernible character, go to school, etc. etc. blah, blah, blah.

Peter, aware that his life was set on a course of dull happiness- (primary school, secondary school, university and then work), decided that this was all rather unfair.

He wanted an adventure that he could write about, but he needed the right environment to write in, so he made a den.

Den 1

The first den was a little make-shift to say the least (though I suppose dens usually are make-shift). It was constructed by placing two chairs (antiqueish) about a Peter length apart, swathed in the finest bed sheet to hand, but it just wasn't conducive to creativity of the magnitude required to conjure up a truly original masterpiece. So he decided to construct a second.

The second, a cardboard box, though large
wasn't exactly inspiring. Peter fashioned some
windows (otherwise known as getting our dad to
cut squares out of the side with a kitchen knife.)
A door was also created using the same technique.
Again this was still a little on the boring side.

The third den was made using the armchair in the living room. He took the cushions from the seat and back and employed them thusly: — The large back cushion was used as the roof, the smaller cushions as roof supports, the seat cushion as the door/drawbridge.

Alas this was too small a space in which to create an adventure comfortably and all he could come up with was clichéd stories about flying carpets and faraway lands. A little role-play was in order to help the creative process along so he decided to go to his dressing up box, thinking this would provide inspiration. Unfortunately, though the box was a

good size and very pretty it did have one small flaw, it was lacking somewhat in content. Being a rather precocious child

(and some have said slightly odd) and with our mother's inability to even thread a needle, he decided to fashion some garments himself. He transformed himself into a Knight in shining armour, Sir Peter of the Garden, Protector of the Plants (what a delusional tool.)

Robin Hood/Peter of Sherwood, stealing from the rich, giving to the poor. He explained to me (though to be honest I didn't care) that Robin Hood had changed his name by deed poll to Peter as King John's men were looking for him.

He couldn't decide who he wanted to be:
A King – King Peter, the Great Emperor of the
Living Room.

A pirate —One Eyed Pete, scourge of the high seas and the bathtub. (I had suggested Paltry Pete, which Peter quite liked the sound of until he asked our mum what paltry actually meant and decided that 'worthless Pete' wasn't quite the image he wished his name to conjure). He had also toyed with, Pandemonium Pete, or One-Eyed Pete with his Parakeet, but felt this was all a little silly.

A bank robber— Baby Pete of the Kitchen table massive.

An executioner—One Chop Peter.

The Grim Reaper— that one didn't really require an additional name, though if it did he would probably be known as Peter the Perisher of Men. Though entertaining, these ideas for

adventures did fall a little short.

It was whilst Peter was plotting for future excitement in his various dens that I was busy making plans of my own – to be fair I was also intending to spoil his fun as well– well what's the function of a sibling at that age if it's not to spoil their brother's plans and schemes. (May I add we do get on now –although more recent events on my part may make things a tad strained family wise for a while, but we will get to that in good time). My designs were more focused on one goal, attaining my grandfather's gingham dressed taxidermy squirrel. Thinking about it, it was a very odd thing for a granddad to have.

Whilst I was failing to attain the ultimate prize (a gingham dressed squirrel) Peter was also struggling, much to my amusement, with his flight of fancy. He felt a fourth den was in order, one with more room than the chair, so the sofa was commissioned. Its construction was of a similar nature to the armchair, but yet again this one fell short. Peter thought hard about how to make a better den. He ventured outside and decided to try and utilise the bush at the end of our garden,

but though it looked ideal from a distance, he found the density of leaves to be inadequate. He would be far too visible.

After a little further scouting Peter decided upon a particularly delightful tree and started to envisage some sort of tree house. He undertook an initial survey (a quick climb and a tug at a few branches to make sure they were secure enough to hold his weight and that of a small wooden structure), the plans were drawn up and construction was started in earnest.

Though it has not been mentioned before, Peter was quite proficient with a hammer and saw and quickly knocked up a delightful little dwelling to house his thoughts.

Charming though it was and fun though it had been whilst in the construction stage and for the initial few days of inhabitancy, it did fall a little short. For a start, usage was limited by our parents, who fretted he might fall and break himself, or that a tramp might take residence in the tree house and kidnap Peter, or that the tree house would become a shelter to some wild animal that would lie in wait and savagely attack Peter whilst he played in it, or that Peter might get wet being outside so much and come down with a cold.

ALL this worrying was stifling his enjoyment of the tree house and therefore stifling his creativity and so he abandoned his dreams of finding wonder in the outdoors and feeling dejected, confined himself to indoor pursuits, hoping that he would be given some creative space to breathe if his parents thought he was safe.

It was around this time that I made my first serious play for the gingham dressed squirrel.

I had made various grabs for the squirrel in the past, in the literal sense at first

whilst being carried by my mum passed the shelf it was living on and by clambering up to nab it, but all attempts up to that point had been quickly thwarted by my parents or grandfather.

I could never reconcile why a normally generous man such as my grandad would deny me, his only granddaughter, my one true desire. Whenever we went to visit him the cupboards would be full of fun things to eat and if he went away on holiday he would always bring back thoughtful little presents, but for some reason he just wouldn't let me have my gingham dream.

I had been scheming for weeks about exactly how to successfully relieve my grandfather of his prized possession. One night, I was having a sleep over at my grandads, which was always fun as it meant eating naughty food for dinner and breakfast and more time to look longingly at the squirrel. As luck would have it Peter was away on a school trip, so there would be no interference from that one. I lay in bed and waited until nightfall (or in other words until my grandad went to asleep). I sneaked down the stairs (avoiding the creaky ones) in to the living room and nabbed my beloved. The appropriation of the squirrel was a relatively quick process. In the squirrel's place I popped what in retrospect was a less than convincing replacement in the form of a soft toy squirrel.

That night I slept in the fabric tented den my grandad had made for me, I must have thought it a great hide out or perhaps it was the sense of excitement at finally having the squirrel in my arms, not having to have to hide it as I would if I were in my bed. I woke early and squirreled the squirrel away (yes I went there) in my bag, planning to casually take my new acquisition back home and secrete it in wardrobe in a little space I had created for it.

Peter, back from his school trip had been picked up by my dad on the way to my grandads to collect me. It was Peter who first noticed the replacement. "Why's Eleanor's squirrel up there instead of grandad's? AAAAAAh has she done a swap?"

My heart sank, no one else had noticed the replacement, why would they? The gingham clad squirrel had been placed so high up that they didn't think I'd be able to get it and they hadn't even thought to look, that was until my little brother came along– why couldn't my dad have picked him up after me? Why was he so annoying? Why was he even born? So many questions, but no answers would satisfy the reality of me having to hand over the squirrel, being told off and left with a new mission... to get Peter back.

My brother was having his own problems, which gave me some minor satisfaction. Deeply dissatisfied with the clichéd stories he had so far penned (though he hadn't actually written them down), Peter decided he needed to go on an adventure of his very own. Knowing he wasn't allowed out of the house or back garden, he explored his surroundings. He started his exploration by climbing the stairs to look up the chimneys in the bedrooms, hoping for at least a priest hole but to no avail.

Then hurtled downstairs into the kitchen. He looked –
In the cupboards
Under the sink
Down the loo

But absolutely nowt, zero, zilch, nada.
He knew the likelihood of finding a mystical kingdom was slim but felt certain that something exciting must happen. I 'helped' Peter discover that there was no passage to Narnia through any wardrobe in the house. He had been fairly certain of this beforehand, but I had been so persistent in my insistence that the wardrobe in my room did indeed contain said passage to a mystical land, that Peter climbed in to double check. As he rummaged around to prove the point I locked him in and wedged my bed against the wardrobe door, which I found amazingly amusing, especially as it led to our parents frantically racing around the house and running up and down the street looking for him when he hadn't come down for dinner.

Our parents had become worried when dad went up to remind Peter that dinner was served and asked me if I had seen him. I decided it would be more amusing to reply in the negative, 'No, I've not seen him for hours, I think he said he might run away because you won't let me have the squirrel' (admittedly this wasn't the most considered response or one that even made any sense).

Peter did however feel a little better when a severe punishment was dealt out. He was discovered nearly two hours later when mum went up to my room to ask if I could think where he might be and to see if anyone had called whilst she had been out looking for him.

I had tried to prevent my mum entering the room when she knocked on the door by leaping up from my bed and darting towards the door, making out I was just leaving my room. "Do you want a cup of tea mum? I'm just going down to make one." But mum could see the strange configuration of furniture and my bed and had already started to move into the room to investigate, leading to the discovery of exactly where Peter had 'run off to', or rather where he had been trapped.

The punishment may have been severe but Peter decided that he needed to dole out his own reprisal. He felt quite vindicated when he persuaded me to eat some 'mini chocolate balls,' that were actually peppercorns. He took joy in telling me of what sheer delight it was watching as I rushed to the kitchen sink to spit them out and seeing the yellow slimy saliva dribble out of my gaping mouth. In the grand scheme of things, his was a short lived victory as I plotted my revenge for this and more than that, for the loss of the squirrel at his hands.

The only place Peter hadn't explored in the hope of finding a wondrous secret world was the cellar. The problem, he could see, was that if he did find a wondrous secret world, how would he keep it secret? It would have been relatively easy to keep the discovery hidden from the family if it had been in the house, as he could just pretend he was playing and no one would disturb him, but the cellar was a place he never ventured in to and questions would be asked.

Peter knew I was scared of the cellar so there was little chance of me discovering what he was up to for a good while, but as has already been mentioned, our parents never gave him a moments peace, constantly fretting over his wellbeing (he was the youngest child). Peter therefore needed something to pacify them and yet allow him space and freedom to create. So Harold was called upon to accompany him on his quest. Harold as I've said was a rather peculiar looking chap, not so much a teddy bear, more a strange disproportionate thing with a huge head, small body, bobbly eyes, two long thin arms and two thin legs set wide apart, with small blobby feet like inflated semicircles. Harold sported a grey V-neck jumper, ribbed on the neck, cuffs and hem, grey shorts and a thin tie (all in a school uniform mode of fashion.) As I said, it wasn't that Peter liked playing with his teddy, in fact he never played with a teddy voluntarily but our parents liked the idea, so he went along with it as it meant that they would leave him alone and allow him to get on with things.

I remember him telling me years later that he had always found the lack of natural light in the cellar creatively restrictive. In fact he found the whole environment restrictive: light, air, space, the damp, the musty smell. If Peter was honest with himself it had little if anything to do with the creative drawbacks and more to do with the general ambiance. It was in fact, more that it gave him the heebie jeebies (who ever uses that phrase other than Peter I don't know?) or, the creeps. He was:

Terrified,
Petrified,
He was frightened
And scared
And lots of other things ending in ed, he would recount.

I mean anything could be down there; monsters, goblins, burglars and god knows what vermin and creatures might be crawling around. What if he was locked in, I could have locked him in, I did have form? No, the cellar was not for him, but desperate times call for desperate measures and Peter was desperate to escape the mundane.

However Peter knew that it was safe to go into the cellar without the fear of me locking him in, a temporary peace treaty had been signed after the locking in the wardrobe and the subsequent 'false chocolate' incident, that had resulted in severe penalties enforced by the UN —our parents, He knew in reality that there was little chance of finding wonder in the cellar, but ventured down in the vein hope of discovering a fantastic kingdom full of magic. Creeping down the threadbare rusty red carpeted stairs with trepidation, he tried to keep his mind from straying on to the horrid beasts that might lie in wait for him and instead concentrated on the task in hand... but each stair awakened thoughts of a new terror that might be awaiting him when he finally submerged himself into the cellar's depths. 1,2,3,4,5,6,7,8,9 and ten. He stopped at number ten, the last and largest step.

Holding Harold tightly in one hand, a torch in the other, surveying the dark, dingy space, Peter stood under the weak light bulb attached to the wall.

A voice suddenly pierced through the silence. "I wouldn't if I were you." Startled, Peter jumped back in disbelief and dropped Harold on the head. 'Oi! Watch out!' shouted the rather gruff voice. To Peter's amazement and horror the voice appeared to be coming from the rather odd looking object with bobbly eyes that sported a school uniform, in other words— Harold!

The voice had a peculiar northern man sort of a twang, somewhere between Oldham, Bolton and Manchester, but on occasion and quite unexpectedly, slipping into some kind of Alan Bennet Yorkshireness. It was very strange thought Peter and certainly nothing like

he'd ever heard, but then he hadn't had a soft toy speak to him before. A thousand thoughts flashed through his head. How strange that a soft toy was speaking, how odd that he had such a broad northern accent, certainly not what you'd expect from a small soft toy or any one of that scale. It seemed too deep to have come from him. Why was Harold suddenly talking to him?
How was he talking?
'I can see you're a little surprised,' said Harold.

Peter said nothing, but slowly reached down towards the strangely proportioned talking, fabric thing. Where on earth was this voice coming from Peter wondered, especially as Harold was not in possession of a mouth or any anatomical area that appeared to move when he spoke? But then I suppose you can buy teddy bears and dollies that say "I love you," and he had seen one of my friend's teddies that spoke to her by name, uttering sentences recorded for her by her dad when she was younger. None of these moved their mouths or any other orifice to speak, so if Harold was to speak why should he have to possess such a thing. It was just the small fact that he had never decided to speak before in all the years Peter had had him that was a little alarming, coupled with the fact that this did not appear to be a pre-recorded message and seemed very much as if Harold had just come to life, literally .

Peter, still in a state of confusion and disbelief, let his grip on Harold loosen as he stared with puzzlement at him, dropping him once again on his fabric head. Harold screamed at Peter and in a shrill voice gave a verbal attack. "I know I'm just a ruse to divert attention from you and that you have only taken me to pacify your parents, but really there's no need to be violent. I can't believe you've just dropped me on my flippin head AGAIN!" Peter stood dumbfounded, staring at this odd-looking fabric thing that was now talking to him.

"Well are you going to pick me up or what? it said, 'Come on don't you know it's rude to stare?"

"Look, just pick me up!"

Harold explained that he was possessed and if Peter didn't carry on playing with him he'd pass it onto Peter and Peter would be possessed forever, forced to roam the planet for eternity, an outcast, shunned by friends, family, even his parents. Harold told him that as long as Peter did as he said he'd be fine. "Now pick me up and let's explore the cellar.'" Not knowing what to think, Peter obliged. Holding Harold once again in his left hand, shaking slightly, Peter walked along the concrete floored passage.

P-"So if you're possessed, whom are you possessed by?"

H- "None of your business. Now shut it and let's get on f' god's sake!"

But Peter was unsure where to get on to.

Creeping down the passage, they arrived at the first junction. Stretching ahead of them was the toilet room that had not been re-plumbed with the rest of the house, so lay unused and was now a narrow storage room, lined on the right hand side with two shelves crammed with books collecting moisture. Diagonally from where Peter had positioned himself, was the washing machine and dryer room, which also held unknown treasures and bountiful supplies (otherwise known as where fun food stuffs were kept that were not allowed to be generally consumed by Peter or me). A turn left led to cellar 1, the main room of the cellar. It overflowed with antiquities, vintage pieces, fascinating artefacts, pieces of history, or in other words junk, old things that our parents couldn't quite bear to throw out, or be bothered enough too.

Cellar 1 also contained three options of direction other than back out from whence Peter came. The options: -
1- Out of the bolted door to the mossy green stone steps, ascending to the garden and sight of previous dens of Peters.
2- In to the small room housing the boiler and where other inhabitants included a forklift pallet to keep objects on so they were off the floor and didn't get damp, on which perched two old sky TV dishes, a set of rusting dumbbells and some other rubbish that would never be used again.
3- 'Cellar 2' where Rasputin the rabbit once resided was a fair sized room with the same concrete floor as the others. Rasputin had taken this room as her home after revealing a penchant for eating telephone wires, answer phone and the final straw, the television wire, the little nibbler had been moved wholesale down into 'Cellar 2.'as it was too dangerous outside in the garden with next doors cat, coupled with the scraggy looking foxes which resided in a den next to the garage and she was too naughty to be upstairs in the rest of the house - yes Rasputin is a male name and quite a peculiar choice considering the associations with its most famous owner, but originally it had been believed to be a male of the species and my brother had been allowed to name her (enough said...).

After a brief investigation of all the aforementioned rooms, it was to 'cellar 2' that Peter and Harold headed. The search so far had been futile. His investigation revealed that though there was an abundance of objects in the cellar, most of it was rubbish, in reality the books and foodstuffs were probably the only things that would ever be used.
It had also revealed that (at least on first inspection) there were no burglars, goblins etc, etc, unless they were lying in wait behind the last remaining place Peter and the now possessed Harold hadn't looked.
They stood timidly in front of the small green cupboard like door in the middle of the wall. "What an odd height to put a door" "Come on. What you waiting for?" piped up Harold, who had been quiet for a good while after realising that shouting, "Boo!" though he found it amusing to watch the look of horror on Peter's face, especially when peering into some dark corner of the cellar, invariably ended up with Peter dropping him on his head and the resulting headache that ensued, had, after the tenth "Boo!" become too much to bear.
Peter was waiting because this door represented the last place where potential goblins, gremlins, burglars, kidnappers etc. might be lying in wait. He waited also because he was a little tired from all this searching and because he wasn't quite sure how to get in as the door started at his head height.

Gingerly, Peter and his possessed friend approached the green doored hole in the wall. He jumped up, trying to flip the latch so they could climb in. But even at a stretch he couldn't reach. Some instrument for growth was needed, perhaps a stretching rack, or just a box to stand on. As there was a box full of Christmas decorations to the left of him, Peter decided to go for the box option.

Clambering on to the box that was now positioned directly under the door, a strange feeling came over Peter that something was waiting for him behind that door. He wasn't sure if it was a good or bad thing. He undid the latch and opened the door. Harold climbed in first, or to be more accurate, Peter lifted him in, as Harold lacked bones and muscular tissue for the required movement and force needed to lift himself up, as he was a soft toy. Before Peter had chance to follow, he heard a, "Good God!" coming from what he had intended as his immediate destination, in a familiar northern twang. The voice belonged to Harold. The reason for the outburst was the rather alarming discovery he had made, which greeted Peter's eyes as he peered into the black cavernous coal room. There directly in front of him, stared a pair of eyes or what would have been eyes but were now only sockets. What was staring at Peter, was a skull.

Peter stood dumbfounded. What on earth was a skull doing in the coal room— for that was what the room was? Thoughts started to flash through his head. Maybe this was a pirate's den where bounty had been hidden. The pirates had all died at the bottom of the ocean after a skirmish with the Royal Navy. No one knew about the guard they had left with the bounty, so he died of hunger. Or maybe the last coal man got trapped in there and no one bothered to look for him as hardly anyone uses coal any more. Maybe it was the remains of an old owner of the house who had been buried alive. Maybe his dad had killed someone, dragged them down to the cellar and buried them. Maybe he had lulled them down and then killed them. Maybe it was the last owner of the house his dad had killed so that he could have the house, after all Peter hadn't seen her since she 'moved out.' Though this was unlikely as his dad wasn't the violent type. But then who knows, they always say it's the

ones you least expect and his dad was very mild mannered, as was his mum. Perhaps she did it. Maybe a serial killer lived in hiding there and this was where he dragged his victims. Maybe someone like Peter had been searching for adventure too and had been locked in by a ghost and never got out and this was all that was left. Maybe the house was on an old burial site and the dead were rising to take back their land. Maybe Peter was next! With this sudden realisation, Peter shot back, flying off the box he had been standing on, falling to the floor with a bump and scurrying for the exit.

But the door was locked. Frantically he tugged at the handle, furiously wrenching at it, whilst shooting glances back at the now open coal room. He screamed for help as he threw himself against the door.

The room felt like it was getting smaller. There was less air. It was closing in. Peter was banging and thumping on the door, hurling himself at it, screaming, tears running down his face, 'Please, PLEASE! MUM! DAD! Eleanor! PLEASE! HELP ME! He shrank into the corner. There was no sound of response. The door seemed to be calling, willing him towards it, taunting him with his fate, mocking him. 'PLEASE! PLEASE! MUM! DAD! Eleanor! PLEASE! HELP MEEE!' But no one, it seems, could hear his screams. The black of the coal room, a chamber of death enveloped him like a coffin, beckoning him, pulling at him; an open mouth waiting to devour its next meal, a meal in which Peter was the main course. Still hammering with his fist, he heard the sound of footsteps 'Help! HELP! IM LOCKED IN!' The footsteps came closer, but as they came closer Peter started to wonder whether they were the footsteps of a friend or foe. Were they the footsteps of his rescuer or of the inhabitant of the cellar? Were they the footsteps of the last person Peter would ever see? Were they the footsteps of a murderer? As the footsteps approached, Peter clung to the wall.

The door opened and Peter flung himself through it and hurtled past me, knocking me to the floor.

Stumbling passed the clutter of the cellar, into the passageway, he scrambled up the threadbare stairs

 "What you think you're doing you little freak! Pushing me out of the way like that! I was only LETTING YOU OUT! You ungrateful midget," I said in a not so comforting tone.

Peter flew towards my dad's legs. He cowered in the corner looking cautiously at the possessed problem, Harold, as our dad stroked his hair with his hand. It was all too much, a possessed toy, finding a skull in the cellar, being trapped, being pursued. It was too much. He tried to explain to our dad what had happened but the words just wouldn't come out. Our dad looked down at him with his big blue friendly eyes, the sky blue colour of Manchester City's' old home kit. With his big arms dad picked him up, "Come on let's see what's down there." But Peter didn't fancy going down to check. He had, had quite enough of that cellar. "Right well I'll go and see then," but this too did not fill Peter with any warmth or reassurance, only fear, for what might happen to our dad if he went down there. After some deliberation it was decided that Peter and the possessed one would stand at the top of the stairs with our mum, dad would go down and investigate whilst whistling 'City, Manchester City, we are the boys that never give in!' so they knew he was alright.

Our dad's exploration yielded no skull and it was concluded that either Peter had imagined it or that it had been there but somehow it now was not, which was pretty much Peters original conclusion before the involvement of our parents, but never mind.

Now on to the rather perplexing problem of the possessed.
Harold had eventually admitted that he had put the skull there after
getting it from the medical student next door. Peter immediately saw a
few problems with this explanation. He wondered how exactly a soft toy,
unable to move of his own free will, had managed to plant a skeleton in
the cellar and how exactly had his possessed soft toy struck up a
reasonable enough friendship with the neighbours to borrow such a valuable
thing?
On asking Harold this, Harold retorted that he could move very well. It
was just that he could only move on his own when no one was looking.
There was a flood of other questions just begging to be asked in response
to this little gem of a response but they would have to wait.

Peter didn't want to go back into the coal room but Harold promised that
he had not put anything else there. Though there had undoubtedly been
much excitement, the fact remained that no secret, mystical, fantastical,
lands had been found. In fact the voyage had wielded so little that the
discovery of a colony of ants would have caused excitement and near
hysteria. The simple fact remained that there was not and probably had
not, ever been a hidden vortex to another dimension, no door to an
enchanted world, but there were few other options for adventure, so it
was to the coal room that Peter now went. The time had come to take
matters in to his own hands, the time had come for Peter to build his own
fantastical, mystical, stupendous, land and the coal room would be the
ideal space for this.
Desperate for adventure, Peter and
Harold climbed in, well, more Peter
climbing with Harold tucked under
his arm). "I hope you've used
deodorant!" Harold said.
Peter ignored him and clambered in. Walking
inside, he felt scared and excited.
He found a dead bird in the back of one
of the rooms. Harold thought they should
keep it as a pet— Peter did not.
He drew up plans for a world of wonderment and started toying with a
variety of mediums to execute it, but decided cardboard was the easiest
to get his hands on and disguise.

He told our parents that he needed cardboard for a project and in addition used the boxes in the cellar still full of books and other bits and bobs from the house move three years before. Using masking tape, duct tape, cardboard, pens and paint, he could create his own little world. His first task was to fashion a den to use as the nerve centre of his operations, somewhere he could manufacture a land the likes no one has ever seen before and also somewhere to hide in, as the coal room was rather scary.

Den number2 the cardboard experiment he had made right at the start of his adventures suddenly sprang to mind as ideal for this and luckily he had had the foresight not to throw it away. Though it had not been conducive to the creative process before, things were different now. The simplicity of its form would not detract from future designs and the sinister aesthetic of the coal room. It was in essence functional, practical and none invasive; it talked the problem and yet was not confrontational. To the outside world it would look like a simple child's den, nothing more, nothing less, yet

inside would be the very nerve centre of operations. Operation centre – 'Make a land– Den2' also offered the advantage of immediacy, it was already constructed, all that was needed was its transportation to the proposed sight. In essence 'Den2' was the very zeitgeist of this whole operation (though he felt zeitgeist was the incorrect word Peter loved it's sound and it seemed appropriate to him for such an endeavour). It had been constructed right at the start of Peter's journey of discovery, it was a symbol of Peters pro–activeness, he wasn't going to wait around for a hidden land just to fall in to his lap, he went out to find one and when he couldn't find one he decided to make his own. 'Den2' was no fancy tree house bought at a garden centre, or showy plastic prefabricated Wendy house, 'Den2' was making the best of what you've got using creative mastery. Yes 'Den2' was perfect, or at least adequate for the time being, it was something to get him going). He felt safe in his little box where he could peep out of the windows and close the cardboard door behind him. He drew and cut out the landscape and made tiny card people in his little cardboard box home.

It was coming to
the end the summer holidays,
though you may have
noticed from the
illustrations that Peter seems
permanently dressed in school   uniform
even when in fancy dress, this was in-fact
just one of his peculiarities and is probably best
just skirted over. The question of Harold, more
precisely what to do with and about Harold was
on Peter's mind. The possessed one was, as
expected, keen to go with Peter to school and
Peter, at his wits end, wanted to explain the
Harold situation to John, his best friend who
had been away on holiday and was due to get
back the night before school started on the
Monday.

Feeling much too mature to play with, or worse, be seen with a soft toy,
Peter hid Harold, much to Harold's consternation in the bottom of his school bag.
Peter arranged to meet John at playtime so he could discretely brief him.
Peter and John sat in a quiet corner near the tree in the playground.
Peter took Harold out cautiously looking around to make sure no one saw him
and placed the possessed before them, but Harold said nothing.
Sympathetically John suggested Harold might just be shy and that they should
try again once he was more use to him.

Simon a fellow class 'mate' had noticed Peter and John sneaking off and ever the inquisitive fellow decided to investigate. Political correctness would dictate that we don't describe the aesthetics of Simon the school bully, but you can form your own opinion from the illustration provided... Simon specialised in a particular brand of torment which he used to make himself feel better for his hideous appearance but also because he was a nasty little... Simon peered down from the branches of the tree he had somehow climbed and could see below Peter and John attempting to engage Harold in conversation.

Simon delighted in spreading the rumour that Peter still played with dolls and that he even thought they spoke to him and that he was a loser and had no friends so had to make them up.

Devastated by the torment of his class 'mates' Peter stopped taking Harold to school and tried pretending he was ill so he didn't have to go to school because he was so embarrassed.

It's not like he was even completely convinced that Harold was speaking and that it wasn't some elaborate pre-recording. The only problem was that every time Peter tried to investigate Harold for a planted device, Harold would let out a scream saying, "I'd thank you to keep your dirty little hands to yourself, you funny little urchin," and Peter felt a little uneasy probing any more. None of the other children understood. They all thought he was making it up, some even said he was a 'crazy lady' which was a tag he was certainly not keen on for all sorts of reasons. Even John, who had tried to stick up for Peter, had started to not want to be associated with him and had recently started to join in with the others for fear of reprisals.

The problem was that not only did everyone think Peter still played with toys, but that Harold had started to mimic Peter's voice (which invariably lead to Peter getting in to trouble), saying things that were inappropriate, rude or immature, but generally a nice little combination of all three.

I later found out that Peter had for some time suspected that I was somehow behind the whole Harold talking thing. But why did he suspect me of being behind Harold talking?
– Did he think he had overhead me saying something?
–Had John, whose sister was one of my friends and class mates, overheard us talking about it and suspected I had been up to something?
– Had I let slip something in conversation, which I should not have known about, that only Harold and John had heard?
–Had it sounded like there was background noise when Harold talked?
– Had I acted strangely, or had a knowing smile on my face when asking how school was going?
–Or had I said anything like "I've heard from John's sister that you think your teddy's still talking to you, you loser and that all the kids in your class hate you"?

Well no, the only real thing that Peter had was the fact I was in the cellar shortly after Harold had found his voice and that I had been on hand to release him from the locked room when normally the last thing I would be doing was going in to the cellar, I was normally even more scared than Peter. The only thing that could overwhelm my fear of anything normally was if it somehow adversely affected Peter. As Peter would tell me much later, he had no idea how or if I was involved, only a strong suspicion that I was.

He was reluctant to open Harold up because that would give the game away. The only way to find out was by investigating my room. This was easier said than done because whenever I was not in it, I kept it locked and there were few times when he was in the house when I wasn't and even fewer when he was in the house and could leave Harold in his room and be free to roam about without our parents worrying.

The only solution was to execute the raid at night when our parents were both asleep. There was slim chance of being able to rummage around my room whilst I was asleep and not wake me. This would lead to me either realising he was on to me or at the very least incurring my wrath. Peter knew he had to bide his time and wait until I was staying at a friend's for the night.

Shortly after Peter's suspicions became heightened, I was sleeping over at a friend's house. I had locked my room, as I always did, however, Peter knew of the spare key that was kept in our

mother's dressing gown pocket, hanging on the back of the door of our parent's bedroom. Peter sneaked into their room

whilst they slept and slid his hand into the pocket. He crept over to my room and quietly unlocked the door. He looked all over. He searched under the bed, in the drawers, in the dreaded wardrobe, on the shelves, in my old doll's house, but nothing, diddily squat. Somewhat disheartened, Peter sat on the bed. He had expected to find elaborate plans linking me inextricably to the whole thing, but there seemed to be none. He could just picture me performing some kind of voodoo or witchcraft over Harold, some spell to bring him to life and to cause Peter consternation. Perhaps I had made a miniature version of Harold to perform witchcraft on, or even a photograph or drawing, with symbols written around it. But he found no signs, not even a book on witchcraft, or potions, nor a cauldron, which he was particularly surprised about, as he had always thought of me as a little witch. He had envisioned finding a fantastical hidden room where monitors, scanners and an array of high tech equipment helped me in my evil quest, but there were none. He imagined that he would at least find a monitor and a walkie-talkie, but there was nothing.

Despondently he sat on the bed. Suddenly he remembered seeing a box in one of my bedroom drawers that he had not given any particular thought to until now. Climbing down from the bed, he walked to the drawer he had been rummaging through only moments before and had discounted because it was full of old nail varnishes, lipsticks, a few sweet wrappers and a box that once contained a mobile phone- nothing unusual. I had always liked to collect nail varnish and lipstick. The sweet wrappers were probably from some secret trip to the shops on the way home from school with a friend. They would have been gorged on at home, but the empty wrappers placed in the draw instead of the bin for fear our mum finding out, as sweets and chocolates were banned,

"It's for your own good. You don't want to end up with teeth like mine." The mobile phone box did not seem strange. I had been given one in case of emergencies and though Peter did think it a little ridiculous someone so young having one, it was not uncommon and many paranoid parents in the area had done the same, not realising that on the off chance their child was somewhere dodgy, that producing a mobile phone would probably increase the chance of them being mugged tenfold. However what had caught Peter's eye was that this box was for a different phone than the one I used, one that he had not seen me with at all, a Smartphone, a rather fancy looking model that looked more suited to a spy film than a schoolgirl. Opening the box Peter was met by a wodge of instruction booklets, chargers, wires to connect to a computer and all the usual paraphernalia and assortment of stuff you get with a mobile phone. Though youthful in age, Peter was quite precocious in every way. Unfortunately though, he was dyslexic. prisons and the 'arts' have the highest proportion of dyslexics by the way which probably accounted for his rather advanced creativity for his age, but it did have its drawbacks when it came to reading instruction books. Although always willing to give reading a bash, he felt that on matters of such importance, a more accurate reader was required. One who would not misread a keyword wrongly all the way through a text and so completely misunderstand the entire context. Or one who wouldn't be reading a passage, then suddenly lose his place, especially when changing line and spend about five minutes trying to re find his place and having forgotten what he was reading.

A ruler over the top of the sentence he was reading did help, unlike the much-feted coloured acetates over passages, that his teacher seemed to think was the cure for dyslexia. She had attended a seminar on the subject and slightly misunderstood the idea that it only helped occasionally and even then it was only with certain types of dyslexia.

(To be fair to her, this was probably because of the rather opinionated teacher in the seminar who sat next to her and kept babbling on under his breath that they need to help themselves and that if people are allowed to use dyslexia as an excuse, they will use it for everything and become lazy and not capable of dealing with the real life.' If you let them get away with saying I forgot to come to class because I'm dyslexic, then how are they going to deal with the real world. If they were looking after a baby they'd remember to feed it wouldn't they, so it's the same principle and though it was explained to him that those are very different things and that primary school children are unlikely to be in such a situation, he had managed to sufficiently distract those around him so much that no one came out of the seminar with a complete grasp of the concepts, yet all had certificates of attendance and fact sheets, that none had time to read because of all the other work and extra courses they were supposed to attempt). Anyway as I was saying, Peter knew he needed help to understand the instructions and was contemplating who he could turn to, certainly not our parents, they'd tell me off and though that would be fun for him to witness there was far more pleasure to be gained from this. Any way how did he know that the additional mobile had anything to do with the whole Harold talking thing? For a start you'd need someone to answer the phone and how was that possible if the phone was inside Harold? Perhaps Peter could ask a friend, but who and how would he be able to take the instructions away without me noticing?

Similarly how would he get the instructions back into my room and in to my drawer? And what if this wasn't the key to Harold speaking? When would he get another opportunity to get into my room to search again?

However, flicking through the instruction book and looking at the annotated picture area, it became apparent that he was in fact barking up the right tree. Though Peter had never seen anything like it, which was hardly surprising as he had little interest in technology, unlike nearly everyone else on the planet, it seemed, the phone could be activated by another device, a mother phone, by using a code in front of the phone number that only I would know. This would allow the phone to act as some sort of fancy walkie-talkie with a video link. He discovered that I had been 'playing' Harold through the use of the mobile phone, presumably planted inside him and activated by my phone.

Peter had expected something much more elaborate than a mobile phone being responsible for bringing Harold to life, but at the same time was surprised at how costly the whole scheme was. How on earth did a schoolgirl afford to fund two Smartphones? The answer was not long in coming, when he lifted up the box that had contained the phone he found, underneath an A5 bulging envelope. Which rather conveniently for him, held information telling him exactly how I had funded it.

Inside were various bank details similar to those Peter himself had seen and been given. They were the details of one of two accounts that had simultaneously been set up after the death of our grandmother. In her will she had stipulated that some of the inheritance our parents received, should be placed in high interest accounts in mine and Peter's names. They could be drawn on when we went to university, or failing that, at a time when most needed such as when buying a house. The details of the accounts were kept in an envelope, in a file, in a box, in a drawer, in a cupboard, in a room, in the cellar. To Peter's knowledge, this was where they stayed. The accounts could only be drawn on when both of us reached a certain age. It was now apparent that the account details had not remained in an envelope, in a file, in a box, in a cupboard, in a room, in the cellar. They were in fact in my drawer, in my room. And from looking at the account details, rather a lot of the money had been withdrawn, blowing the theory that we could not access the money pre- university age. In fact looking through the rest of the papers and receipts, it was blatantly obvious that it was not only Peter who was in the dark over the withdrawal. This deduction was simple as having known our parents all his life; he knew that they would not see a shopping spree as a suitable reason to access funds that had been created with the aforementioned stipulations. I had purchased, handbags, shoes and make up as well as two mobile phones. A large amount of the remaining money had been spent on telephone bills. The clever little game I had been playing, had been a rather expensive one financially and if Peter had his way it would also prove to be expensive in so many other ways, as he prepared to wreak his revenge.

Before Peter could start fully planning the revenge, he needed to check that he was right. There was only one way to do this. He would have to dissect Harold. Keen not to let it be known that he had discovered my little game, until he was certain of the actions he would take in response,

he knew that he could not simply go to his room where he had left Harold and with a swift flourish wielding the sharpened edge of a knife, thrust it in to the fabric belly and into the wadding below. This of course would have given temporary satisfaction but the short-lived excitement could well be at the expense of future gain if he was discovered. The distinct possibility of me turning on the phone and finding him mid plunge was too great. Peter needed to employ a far more subtle excavation and exploration.

Carefully taking a scalpel (where exactly he got this from is not entirely known)

he crept up behind Harold as he slept and with one neat
incision, drew the knife down. Something that surprised Peter
was that Harold had not noticed this at all, which if he had
been alive you would expect someone cutting in to you to
have at least registered an 'Ooh!' especially from such a
vocal little chap; this was the thing though, Harold only
noticed Peter when Peter was making noise or was in his
eye line. Most people would sense the presence of someone
in a room, where as Harold seldom did, yet another reason for
Peter to believe that perhaps there was something not quite
right about the whole possessed notion that Harold had
suggested to him.

The incision had been made and carefully Peter peered in;
there in front of him was the glint of something familiar and
with the gentlest of tugs out popped the aforementioned
phone as had been expected.

The Act of Revenge

After carefully placing the phone back into Harold and subtly re-stitching him, Peter crept out of his room. Running down into the cellar, he felt the time had come to stop using his den as the nerve centre of his 'world' and turn it into the headquarters for operation 'get Eleanor (aka me) back.'

Peter's Possible Plans for Revenge

There were myriad possibilities that he initially came up with. He could: —

-Shave my head
-Feed me rat poison
-Tell everyone at school I still wet the bed
-Tell everyone I had nits
- Set fire to me as I slept

But his favoured option and indeed the one he eventually employed, promised to yield amusing results, with crucially, little chance of reprisal from our parents or me. It was quite possible neither would ever find out what he had done. The idea was that he would go on pretending he didn't know about my deception, whilst at the same time, telling all sorts of things to Harold that he had supposedly heard other children and their parents saying about me. Peter's fabrications would go unnoticed as I wouldn't be able to tell anyone what had been said, or my initial deception would be discovered. This in turn would increase my anxieties.

And he was right, a subtle comment here, a whisper there, all told to Harold in 'confidence.' Tiny things, like that the own clothes day at school has been cancelled, so I turned up in my school uniform; leading to all my classmates teasing me as they were all in their ordinary clothes. They called me a geek for wanting to wear my uniform. Some said I was a tramp for not being able to afford the £1 for the own clothes day. Some said that I had nothing to wear.

Seeing the success of his trick, Peter decided to step it up a notch. To turn up the gas, he decided to target me psychologically. One ploy that he thought might yield dividends, was to comment on my weight or complexion, or more specifically pretend that he had overheard others commenting that I looked chubby or spotty, and that Peter thought it was really mean and that I was going through an awkward growth stage. (A double whammy. Make me feel guilty because Peter was sticking up for me and bad because people thought all sorts of horrid things about me). I was trapped; if I questioned Peter or even suggested I had heard him, my game would be up. He would stop telling Harold all his 'secrets' and I needed the knowledge. Frustrated and hurt, I began to resent my friends. It became a real hatred. Why were they being so nasty behind my back? I felt victimised and ostracized. I couldn't tell my parents or teachers because no one had said or acted any differently to my face. If it came out I had found out through Harold that I had planted a mobile phone in him to play a trick on Peter, it was doubtful I would get any sympathy and in fact much more likely my life would become a whole lot worse, especially when they found out how I had been funding it. In fact, the severity of the situation had only really dawned on me. I knew I'd be in trouble if our parents found out, but had only really thought of the delight of tricking my weird, irritating little brother and making his life hell.

Why had I spent so much time and money on trying to trick the little urchin? I knew I was stuck and Peter was fully aware of all the above.

Whilst all of this was going on I had not forgotten my greatest challenge- that of attaining the squirrel, indeed one of the ultimate aims of this deception had been to, in the long term, manipulate Peter so much that he would steal the squirrel for me, but as I say this was a long term plan and one that seemed to be ever diminishing in likelihood, so in the meantime I made a few attempts myself to attain the gingham one.

My next 'great idea' for squirrel triumph was to fake a break in at my grandads. Another sleep over was to be my time to strike but this time it was all planned out to what I thought was near perfection.
Again I waited for my granddad and this time Peter, who was also staying over, to go to bed and once again I sneaked down stairs, wearing gloves and plastic covers over my shoes, to retrieve my ginger furred obsession. But instead of leaving a feeble excuse of a replica I opened the back door picked up a stone that I

covered with fabric to reduce the noise and smashed one of the panes of glass in the patio door; opened the door and crept back in. I'd brought a black bag with me that I planned to put bits and bobs of no particular value in.- I wasn't trying to be malicious I just wanted it to look like a real break in and draw away any link to me as it would have if it was only the squirrel that went missing. All was going well. I obviously prioritised the seizure of the squirrel, then sporadically picked up various objects and put them in the bag. I intended to hide the bag in plain sight in the garden and make it look like the 'thief' had been disturbed and dumped the booty and had only been able to take a few less valuable things, obviously the squirrel, as well as a funny porcelain ornament that had been given to my grandfather years ago and he hadn't had the heart to chuck and that bloody ugly clock that I'd been trying to 'accidentally' drop and break for years.

All was going to plan, that is until Peter came down mid 'break in'. He crept in so quietly I didn't even notice him until I realised there was an extra object in the bag and I looked around and saw him , startled he said ' Sorry I put that one in there, I wasn't sure what the game was so I just started to put stuff in'. I won't bore you with how this played out but needless to say... not well... and it can be filed under another unsuccessful attempt to gain the squirrel.

I would love to say there was a great conclusion from the phone planting saga; eventually I discovered what I had suspected, that Peter had known it was me who was behind Harold's miraculous 'coming to life'. Neither of us said anything, neither would admit such things at that age to each other. It was only last year that it all came out after a few too many drinks when I was back for Christmas; we did laugh about it, both a little bitterly on remembering certain details. But we were both young and knew that sibling rivalries could easily escalate out of hand. We held no real grudges. Well Peter didn't, he was always a little better at these things than me... I said I didn't hold any grudges, so I suppose I was half way there and I think at the time he believed me.

But Peter's childhood revenge, through his spiteful whispers to Harold about what he had supposedly heard other children say about me; and my subsequent adverse reaction mentally and physically did serve to help me reconcile my final methods in attaining the gingham clad squirrel.

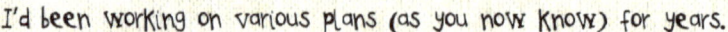

Age 20 the final plan- at last success- yesterday:

Looking back now on yesterday's events it feels more like a film I have watched than something I was part of and more distant that any of the events I've been telling you about from my childhood. Hazy is probably the most accurate way of describing the memories of how it all happened. I'd planned it of course; I'd been working on various plans (as you now know) for years.

It's funny really that I'm telling you of all people about this, but they say it's easier to confide in those less familiar.

A combination of elation and melancholy washes over me each time I look at the splendidly curious object in my hands. For so long I had desired that squirrel that I think if truth be told I have forgotten what it was that made me crave it so much.

I liken it to an elite athlete, from a young age you strive to achieve the seemingly unattainable, to win the ultimate trophy. Hours of practice, of failed bids, of psychological turmoil and warfare go in to attaining the one objective, that when finally one 'glorious' sweat stained day- pushed to the brink of physical and mental exhaustion, you finally win and have the prize in your hands, it is hard to remember exactly why you wanted it in the first place and the achievement of your goal leaves you feeling a little hollow, because what else is there to achieve, what else is there to focus on?

I had dreamt up all sorts of elaborate plans and schemes for relieving my grandfather of the gingham one, but ultimately the only way I could see the victory being a long lasting one, without fear of having to give the squirrel back, was if grandpapa popped his clogs and there seemed little chance of that anytime soon- he was a wily old fella that one.

When I was younger I would always jump out trying to shock my grandad to see if he would keel over. I tried all sorts of ever more elaborate surprises, but nothing worked, he just saw it as me playing around and laughed.

AS I grew older though, I realised it would be best if it seemed like his death wasn't my fault.

When Peter annoyed me and particularly during the troublesome Harold period, I fantasised about somehow getting rid of my grandad and framing my brother. You could say killing two birds with one stone, well Peter would still be alive, so technically one bird but he would certainly go away for a good while.

When Peter and I went away to university, Peter would sometimes visit our grandad on his own and stay over. For some reason those two were always a little closer than I was with either of them; perhaps it was because I continually tried to steal from my grandad and kept on trying to get my brother in trouble, who can say.

With this in mind, I thought it would be fun to travel up to my grandad's house in disguise sometime when Peter was staying there. I would pop my granddad off in his sleep then make it look like Peter had done it— maybe I could slip Peter some sleeping pills so he wouldn't disturb me, then I could plant some illegal substances in his bedroom at our grandfathers and beforehand in his room at our parents, to make it look like he had some sort of addiction and was unhinged. I could make it look like Peter had stolen some stuff to feed his addiction. Maybe I could also plant my grandfather's fancy watch and some money on him to add authenticity; then I could take the squirrel.
It seemed a great idea — off with grandad and Peter too (to prison).
The only real thing to decide was how to get my hands on the squirrel, would I wait until the will was read and hope to inherited her; well that was ripe with problems. What if it was left for someone else, I would have the faff of having to get rid of them as well?
If I nab the squirrel there and then after relieving my grandfather of his existence, wouldn't that just make me look suspicious? Was there not a way I could take the squirrel there and then and be beyond suspicion? I wracked my brain around that one for so long it made my head spin.

Anyway let's not worry now how I got myself around those problems, not that I'm incriminating myself by admitting that I did, all you need to know is that all is good with the world, well to an extent. I have the squirrel now and that's the main thing.

It's such a pity I snagged the squirrel's gingham dress and that spot of blood that wouldn't come out was bound to bring up questions. Maybe I could use some specialist stain remover. I do rather like the effect of the tear in the dress where the ruffles now peak out, it makes it feel a little more avant-garde or something, the only problem was that it was a tad incriminating, especially due to how it happened, but let's not dwell on that, the main thing is that I finally have the gingham clad squirrel in my arms.

Also by David Longshaw

DAVID LONGSHAW
PRESENTS
MILDRED

A fashionable children's tale for grown-ups

Maude the fashion fabric mouse introduces you to Mildred (the peculiar penguin who sees people as dresses) in David Longshaw's debut book.

DAVID LONGSHAW

PRESENTS

MAUDE

A fashionable children's tale for grown-ups

I said to her, I said: 'Doris, no! You've got your own, stop trying to nick mine; you're always angling after what's mine. If it's not me Balenciaga hand bag, it's me David Longshaw dress, or me Chanel lipstick (I mean, who shares a lipstick? It's not hygienic!), and if it's not that, it's me Manolo's and more often than not it's me **sodding sticky bun** or scone!'

Meet Maude the 32cm fabric fashion mouse

Join her in her quest to find a home OF HER OWN and in her battle to conquer the fashion world in fashion designer and illustrator David Longshaw's second book in the Maude and Doris series, Maude, A fashionable children's tale for grown-ups!

www.ingramcontent.com/pod-product-compliance
Lightning Source LLC
Chambersburg PA
CBHW050822290526
45792CB00001B/218